CW00461067

the
reinvent
Daily Log

by chris farrell

Achieve more in the next 6 weeks
than you have in the last 6 years.

PLEASE NOTE:

This Daily Log is to accompany the training
found at ProjectReinventYourself.com

Copyright © 2022 Project Reinvent Yourself | Chris Farrell

All rights reserved.

No part of this publication may be reproduced, distributed, or transmitted in any form or by any means, including photocopying, recording, or other electronic or mechanical methods, or by any information storage and retrieval system without the prior written permission of the publisher, except in the case of very brief quotations embodied in critical reviews and certain other noncommercial uses permitted by copyright law.

INTRODUCTION

Hi, it's Chris Farrell here.

Thanks so much for grabbing your copy of the reinvent Daily Log.

PLEASE NOTE:

Before we jump in, please let me remind you that this Daily Log is designed to accompany the training that you will find inside ProjectReinventYourself.com

If you have not gone through the training yet, this Daily Log may not make sense! So please look at the training before going any further.

The entire purpose of this Daily Log is to give you a tried and tested SYSTEM that will allow you to reinvent your life.

Remember…it's ok to start over!

We can all get 1 percent better every day.

We can all begin the process to get back on track.

We can all be a slightly better person today than we were yesterday.

This reinvent DAILY LOG will show you how.

It's great to have you here.

Let's begin.

READ EVERY DAY

My life is a consequence of my actions and decisions.

My outcomes are a lagging measure of my habits.

I don't know how strong I can become.

What would happen if I really ran hard for one year?

Thoreau said 'many people live lives of quiet desperation, taking their song within them to the grave'.

Discipline is the route to change. It does however require letting go of sloth and laziness.

Imagine the woman/man I can be and work single handedly at that. I can be so much more than I currently am. But this will take courage.

The elusive holy grail of human existence is the ability to rewire one's own brain to embrace this COURAGE and to continually do better – regardless of my feelings, external conditions or motivational state.

Remember - you do not rise to the level of your goals – you fall to the level of your systems. Self-improvement takes self-discipline.

The path to success arises through embracing pain and fear – not by avoiding them.

The quality of my life is in direct correlation to my habits.

My goal is to get 1% better everyday.

Date:	What Is My WHY?
Quote:	

Top Priority for Today		Top Priority for Tomorrow
	Achieved? ☐ Yes ☐ No If no – why?	

3 Daily Habits

Stretch		Gratitude		Hydrate	
Achieved?	Day nos:	Achieved?	Day nos:	Achieved?	Day nos:
☐ Yes No ☐		☐ Yes No ☐		☐ Yes No ☐	

GOALS: specific projects	Deadline Date	Days left?	Yes/No?
GOAL 1:			
GOAL 2:			

3 Wins of the Day

Daily Self Improvement (what did I learn today?)

Do I count today as a successful day? ☐ Yes   ☐ No

By the end of the day I want to be **a tiny bit better** than I was this morning || What have I **LEARNED** today || Don't Waste Time ||
Make Yourself Into Something || You're not everything you could be and you KNOW it || The #1 skill to develop is **COURAGE**

Date:	What Is My WHY?
Quote:	

Top Priority for Today		Top Priority for Tomorrow
	Achieved? ☐ Yes ☐ No If no – why?	

3 Daily Habits

Stretch		Gratitude		Hydrate	
Achieved?	Day nos:	Achieved?	Day nos:	Achieved?	Day nos:
☐ Yes No ☐		☐ Yes No ☐		☐ Yes No ☐	

GOALS: specific projects	Deadline Date	Days left?	Yes/No?
GOAL 1:			
GOAL 2:			

3 Wins of the Day

Daily Self Improvement (what did I learn today?)

Do I count today as a successful day? ☐ Yes   ☐ No

By the end of the day I want to be **a tiny bit better** than I was this morning || What have I <u>LEARNED</u> today || Don't Waste Time ||
Make Yourself Into Something || You're not everything you could be and you KNOW it || The #1 skill to develop is **COURAGE**

Date:	What Is My WHY?
Quote:	

Top Priority for Today		Top Priority for Tomorrow
	Achieved? ☐ **Yes** ☐ **No** **If no – why?**	

3 Daily Habits

Stretch		Gratitude		Hydrate	
Achieved?	Day nos:	Achieved?	Day nos:	Achieved?	Day nos:
☐ **Yes** **No ☐**		☐ **Yes** **No ☐**		☐ **Yes** **No ☐**	

GOALS: specific projects	Deadline Date	Days left?	Yes/No?
GOAL 1:			
GOAL 2:			

3 Wins of the Day

Daily Self Improvement (what did I learn today?)

Do I count today as a successful day? ☐ Yes ☐ No

By the end of the day I want to be **a tiny bit better** than I was this morning || What have I **LEARNED** today || Don't Waste Time ||
Make Yourself Into Something || You're not everything you could be and you KNOW it || The #1 skill to develop is **COURAGE**

Date:	What Is My WHY?
Quote:	

Top Priority for Today		Top Priority for Tomorrow
	Achieved? ☐ Yes ☐ No If no – why?	

3 Daily Habits

Stretch		Gratitude		Hydrate	
Achieved?	Day nos:	Achieved?	Day nos:	Achieved?	Day nos:
☐ Yes No ☐		☐ Yes No ☐		☐ Yes No ☐	

GOALS: specific projects	Deadline Date	Days left?	Yes/No?
GOAL 1:			
GOAL 2:			

3 Wins of the Day

Daily Self Improvement (what did I learn today?)

Do I count today as a successful day? ☐ Yes ☐ No

By the end of the day I want to be **a tiny bit better** than I was this morning || What have I **LEARNED** today || Don't Waste Time ||
Make Yourself Into Something || You're not everything you could be and you KNOW it || The #1 skill to develop is **COURAGE**

Date:	What Is My WHY?
Quote:	

<table>
<tr><td colspan="2" align="center">Top Priority for Today</td><td align="center">Top Priority for Tomorrow</td></tr>
<tr><td></td><td>Achieved?

☐ Yes

☐ No
If no – why?</td><td></td></tr>
</table>

3 Daily Habits

Stretch		Gratitude		Hydrate	
Achieved?	Day nos:	Achieved?	Day nos:	Achieved?	Day nos:
☐ Yes No ☐		☐ Yes No ☐		☐ Yes No ☐	

GOALS: specific projects		Deadline Date	Days left?	Yes/No?
GOAL 1:				
GOAL 2:				

3 Wins of the Day

Daily Self Improvement (what did I learn today?)

Do I count today as a successful day? ☐ Yes ☐ No

By the end of the day I want to be **a tiny bit better** than I was this morning || What have I <u>LEARNED</u> today || Don't Waste Time ||
Make Yourself Into Something || You're not everything you could be and you KNOW it || The #1 skill to develop is **COURAGE**

Date:	What Is My WHY?
Quote:	

Top Priority for Today		Top Priority for Tomorrow
	Achieved? ☐ **Yes** ☐ **No** If no – why?	

3 Daily Habits

Stretch		Gratitude		Hydrate	
Achieved?	Day nos:	Achieved?	Day nos:	Achieved?	Day nos:
☐ **Yes** No ☐		☐ **Yes** No ☐		☐ **Yes** No ☐	

GOALS: specific projects	Deadline Date	Days left?	Yes/No?
GOAL 1:			
GOAL 2:			

3 Wins of the Day

Daily Self Improvement (what did I learn today?)

Do I count today as a successful day? ☐ Yes ☐ No

By the end of the day I want to be **a tiny bit better** than I was this morning || What have I **LEARNED** today || Don't Waste Time ||
Make Yourself Into Something || You're not everything you could be and you KNOW it || The #1 skill to develop is **COURAGE**

Date:	What Is My WHY?
Quote:	

Top Priority for Today		Top Priority for Tomorrow
	Achieved? ☐ Yes ☐ No If no – why?	

3 Daily Habits

Stretch		Gratitude		Hydrate	
Achieved?	Day nos:	Achieved?	Day nos:	Achieved?	Day nos:
☐ Yes No ☐		☐ Yes No ☐		☐ Yes No ☐	

GOALS: specific projects	Deadline Date	Days left?	Yes/No?
GOAL 1:			
GOAL 2:			

3 Wins of the Day

Daily Self Improvement (what did I learn today?)

Do I count today as a successful day? ☐ Yes ☐ No

By the end of the day I want to be **a tiny bit better** than I was this morning || What have I LEARNED today || Don't Waste Time ||
Make Yourself Into Something || You're not everything you could be and you KNOW it || The #1 skill to develop is **COURAGE**

Date:	What Is My WHY?
Quote:	

Top Priority for Today		Top Priority for Tomorrow
	Achieved? ☐ Yes ☐ No If no – why?	

3 Daily Habits

Stretch		Gratitude		Hydrate	
Achieved?	Day nos:	Achieved?	Day nos:	Achieved?	Day nos:
☐ Yes No ☐		☐ Yes No ☐		☐ Yes No ☐	

GOALS: specific projects	Deadline Date	Days left?	Yes/No?
GOAL 1:			
GOAL 2:			

3 Wins of the Day

Daily Self Improvement (what did I learn today?)

Do I count today as a successful day? ☐ Yes   ☐ No

By the end of the day I want to be **a tiny bit better** than I was this morning || What have I **LEARNED** today || Don't Waste Time || **Make Yourself Into Something** || You're not everything you could be and you KNOW it || The #1 skill to develop is **COURAGE**

Date:	What Is My WHY?
Quote:	

Top Priority for Today		Top Priority for Tomorrow
	Achieved? ☐ **Yes** ☐ **No** If no – why?	

3 Daily Habits

Stretch		Gratitude		Hydrate	
Achieved?	Day nos:	Achieved?	Day nos:	Achieved?	Day nos:
☐ **Yes** No ☐		☐ **Yes** No ☐		☐ **Yes** No ☐	

GOALS: specific projects	Deadline Date	Days left?	Yes/No?
GOAL 1:			
GOAL 2:			

3 Wins of the Day

Daily Self Improvement (what did I learn today?)

Do I count today as a successful day? ☐ Yes ☐ No

By the end of the day I want to be **a tiny bit better** than I was this morning || What have I **LEARNED** today || Don't Waste Time ||
Make Yourself Into Something || You're not everything you could be and you KNOW it || The #1 skill to develop is **COURAGE**

Date:		What Is My WHY?
Quote:		

Top Priority for Today | Top Priority for Tomorrow

Top Priority for Today	Achieved? ☐ Yes ☐ No If no – why?	Top Priority for Tomorrow

3 Daily Habits

Stretch		Gratitude		Hydrate	
Achieved?	Day nos:	Achieved?	Day nos:	Achieved?	Day nos:
☐ Yes No ☐		☐ Yes No ☐		☐ Yes No ☐	

GOALS: specific projects		Deadline Date	Days left?	Yes/No?
GOAL 1:				
GOAL 2:				

3 Wins of the Day

Daily Self Improvement (what did I learn today?)

Do I count today as a successful day? ☐ Yes ☐ No

By the end of the day I want to be **a tiny bit better** than I was this morning || What have I **LEARNED** today || Don't Waste Time ||
Make Yourself Into Something || You're not everything you could be and you KNOW it || The #1 skill to develop is **COURAGE**

Date:	What Is My WHY?
Quote:	

Top Priority for Today		Top Priority for Tomorrow
	Achieved? ☐ **Yes** ☐ **No** **If no – why?**	

3 Daily Habits

Stretch		Gratitude		Hydrate	
Achieved?	**Day nos:**	**Achieved?**	**Day nos:**	**Achieved?**	**Day nos:**
☐ **Yes** **No** ☐		☐ **Yes** **No** ☐		☐ **Yes** **No** ☐	

GOALS: specific projects	Deadline Date	Days left?	Yes/No?
GOAL 1:			
GOAL 2:			

3 Wins of the Day

Daily Self Improvement (what did I learn today?)

Do I count today as a successful day? ☐ Yes   ☐ No

By the end of the day I want to be **a tiny bit better** than I was this morning || What have I **LEARNED** today || Don't Waste Time ||
Make Yourself Into Something || You're not everything you could be and you KNOW it || The #1 skill to develop is **COURAGE**

Date:		What Is My WHY?
Quote:		

Top Priority for Today		Top Priority for Tomorrow
	Achieved? ☐ **Yes** ☐ **No** If no – why?	

3 Daily Habits

Stretch		Gratitude		Hydrate	
Achieved?	**Day nos:**	**Achieved?**	**Day nos:**	**Achieved?**	**Day nos:**
☐ Yes No ☐		☐ Yes No ☐		☐ Yes No ☐	

GOALS: specific projects	Deadline Date	Days left?	Yes/No?
GOAL 1:			
GOAL 2:			

3 Wins of the Day

Daily Self Improvement (what did I learn today?)

Do I count today as a successful day? ☐ Yes ☐ No

By the end of the day I want to be **a tiny bit better** than I was this morning || What have I **LEARNED** today || Don't Waste Time ||
Make Yourself Into Something || You're not everything you could be and you KNOW it || The #1 skill to develop is **COURAGE**

Date:	What Is My WHY?
Quote:	

Top Priority for Today		Top Priority for Tomorrow
	Achieved? ☐ Yes ☐ No If no – why?	

3 Daily Habits

Stretch		Gratitude		Hydrate	
Achieved?	Day nos:	Achieved?	Day nos:	Achieved?	Day nos:
☐ Yes No ☐		☐ Yes No ☐		☐ Yes No ☐	

GOALS: specific projects	Deadline Date	Days left?	Yes/No?
GOAL 1:			
GOAL 2:			

3 Wins of the Day

Daily Self Improvement (what did I learn today?)

Do I count today as a successful day? ☐ Yes ☐ No

By the end of the day I want to be **a tiny bit better** than I was this morning || What have I **LEARNED** today || Don't Waste Time ||
Make Yourself Into Something || You're not everything you could be and you KNOW it || The #1 skill to develop is **COURAGE**

Date:	What Is My WHY?
Quote:	

Top Priority for Today		Top Priority for Tomorrow
	Achieved? ☐ **Yes** ☐ **No** If no – why?	

3 Daily Habits

Stretch		Gratitude		Hydrate	
Achieved?	Day nos:	Achieved?	Day nos:	Achieved?	Day nos:
☐ **Yes** No ☐		☐ **Yes** No ☐		☐ **Yes** No ☐	

GOALS: specific projects	Deadline Date	Days left?	Yes/No?
GOAL 1:			
GOAL 2:			

3 Wins of the Day

Daily Self Improvement (what did I learn today?)

Do I count today as a successful day? ☐ Yes ☐ No

By the end of the day I want to be **a tiny bit better** than I was this morning || What have I LEARNED today || Don't Waste Time || **Make Yourself Into Something** || You're not everything you could be and you KNOW it || The #1 skill to develop is **COURAGE**

Date:	What Is My WHY?
Quote:	

Top Priority for Today		Top Priority for Tomorrow
	Achieved? ☐ **Yes** ☐ **No** If no – why?	

3 Daily Habits

Stretch		Gratitude		Hydrate	
Achieved?	**Day nos:**	**Achieved?**	**Day nos:**	**Achieved?**	**Day nos:**
☐ **Yes** No ☐		☐ **Yes** No ☐		☐ **Yes** No ☐	

GOALS: specific projects	Deadline Date	Days left?	Yes/No?
GOAL 1:			
GOAL 2:			

3 Wins of the Day

Daily Self Improvement (what did I learn today?)

Do I count today as a successful day? ☐ Yes ☐ No

By the end of the day I want to be **a tiny bit better** than I was this morning || What have I <u>LEARNED</u> today || Don't Waste Time ||
Make Yourself Into Something || You're not everything you could be and you KNOW it || The #1 skill to develop is **COURAGE**

Date:	What Is My WHY?
Quote:	

Top Priority for Today		Top Priority for Tomorrow
	Achieved? ☐ Yes ☐ No If no – why?	

3 Daily Habits

Stretch		Gratitude		Hydrate	
Achieved?	Day nos:	Achieved?	Day nos:	Achieved?	Day nos:
☐ Yes No ☐		☐ Yes No ☐		☐ Yes No ☐	

GOALS: specific projects	Deadline Date	Days left?	Yes/No?
GOAL 1:			
GOAL 2:			

3 Wins of the Day

Daily Self Improvement (what did I learn today?)

Do I count today as a successful day? ☐ Yes ☐ No

By the end of the day I want to be **a tiny bit better** than I was this morning || What have I **LEARNED** today || Don't Waste Time ||
Make Yourself Into Something || You're not everything you could be and you KNOW it || The #1 skill to develop is **COURAGE**

Date:	What Is My WHY?
Quote:	

Top Priority for Today		Top Priority for Tomorrow
	Achieved? ☐ Yes ☐ No If no – why?	

3 Daily Habits

Stretch		Gratitude		Hydrate	
Achieved?	Day nos:	Achieved?	Day nos:	Achieved?	Day nos:
☐ Yes No ☐		☐ Yes No ☐		☐ Yes No ☐	

GOALS: specific projects	Deadline Date	Days left?	Yes/No?
GOAL 1:			
GOAL 2:			

3 Wins of the Day

Daily Self Improvement (what did I learn today?)

Do I count today as a successful day? ☐ Yes   ☐ No

By the end of the day I want to be **a tiny bit better** than I was this morning || What have I **LEARNED** today || Don't Waste Time ||
Make Yourself Into Something || You're not everything you could be and you KNOW it || The #1 skill to develop is **COURAGE**

Date:	What Is My WHY?
Quote:	

Top Priority for Today		Top Priority for Tomorrow
	Achieved? ☐ Yes ☐ No If no – why?	

3 Daily Habits

Stretch		Gratitude		Hydrate	
Achieved?	Day nos:	Achieved?	Day nos:	Achieved?	Day nos:
☐ Yes No ☐		☐ Yes No ☐		☐ Yes No ☐	

GOALS: specific projects	Deadline Date	Days left?	Yes/No?
GOAL 1:			
GOAL 2:			

3 Wins of the Day

Daily Self Improvement (what did I learn today?)

Do I count today as a successful day? ☐ Yes   ☐ No

By the end of the day I want to be **a tiny bit better** than I was this morning || What have I <u>LEARNED</u> today || Don't Waste Time ||
Make Yourself Into Something || You're not everything you could be and you KNOW it || The #1 skill to develop is **COURAGE**

Date:	What Is My WHY?
Quote:	

Top Priority for Today		Top Priority for Tomorrow
	Achieved? ☐ Yes ☐ No If no – why?	

3 Daily Habits

Stretch		Gratitude		Hydrate	
Achieved?	Day nos:	Achieved?	Day nos:	Achieved?	Day nos:
☐ Yes No ☐		☐ Yes No ☐		☐ Yes No ☐	

GOALS: specific projects	Deadline Date	Days left?	Yes/No?
GOAL 1:			
GOAL 2:			

3 Wins of the Day

Daily Self Improvement (what did I learn today?)

Do I count today as a successful day? ☐ Yes ☐ No

By the end of the day I want to be **a tiny bit better** than I was this morning || What have I <u>LEARNED</u> today || Don't Waste Time || **Make Yourself Into Something** || You're not everything you could be and you KNOW it || The #1 skill to develop is **COURAGE**

Date:	What Is My WHY?
Quote:	

Top Priority for Today		Top Priority for Tomorrow
	Achieved? ☐ Yes ☐ No If no – why?	

3 Daily Habits

Stretch		Gratitude		Hydrate	
Achieved?	Day nos:	Achieved?	Day nos:	Achieved?	Day nos:
☐ Yes No ☐		☐ Yes No ☐		☐ Yes No ☐	

GOALS: specific projects	Deadline Date	Days left?	Yes/No?
GOAL 1:			
GOAL 2:			

3 Wins of the Day

Daily Self Improvement (what did I learn today?)

Do I count today as a successful day? ☐ Yes ☐ No

By the end of the day I want to be **a tiny bit better** than I was this morning || What have I LEARNED today || Don't Waste Time ||
Make Yourself Into Something || You're not everything you could be and you KNOW it || The #1 skill to develop is **COURAGE**

Date:	What Is My WHY?
Quote:	

Top Priority for Today		Top Priority for Tomorrow
	Achieved? ☐ **Yes** ☐ **No** If no – why?	

3 Daily Habits

Stretch		Gratitude		Hydrate	
Achieved?	Day nos:	Achieved?	Day nos:	Achieved?	Day nos:
☐ **Yes** **No** ☐		☐ **Yes** **No** ☐		☐ **Yes** **No** ☐	

GOALS: specific projects	Deadline Date	Days left?	Yes/No?
GOAL 1:			
GOAL 2:			

3 Wins of the Day

Daily Self Improvement (what did I learn today?)

Do I count today as a successful day? ☐ Yes   ☐ No

By the end of the day I want to be **a tiny bit better** than I was this morning || What have I **LEARNED** today || Don't Waste Time ||
Make Yourself Into Something || You're not everything you could be and you KNOW it || The #1 skill to develop is **COURAGE**

Date:	What Is My WHY?
Quote:	

Top Priority for Today		Top Priority for Tomorrow
	Achieved? ☐ Yes ☐ No If no – why?	

3 Daily Habits

Stretch		Gratitude		Hydrate	
Achieved?	Day nos:	Achieved?	Day nos:	Achieved?	Day nos:
☐ Yes No ☐		☐ Yes No ☐		☐ Yes No ☐	

GOALS: specific projects	Deadline Date	Days left?	Yes/No?
GOAL 1:			
GOAL 2:			

3 Wins of the Day

Daily Self Improvement (what did I learn today?)

Do I count today as a successful day? ☐ Yes   ☐ No

By the end of the day I want to be **a tiny bit better** than I was this morning || What have I LEARNED today || Don't Waste Time ||
Make Yourself Into Something || You're not everything you could be and you KNOW it || The #1 skill to develop is **COURAGE**

Date:	What Is My WHY?
Quote:	

Top Priority for Today		Top Priority for Tomorrow
	Achieved? ☐ **Yes** ☐ **No** If no – why?	

3 Daily Habits

Stretch		Gratitude		Hydrate	
Achieved?	Day nos:	Achieved?	Day nos:	Achieved?	Day nos:
☐ **Yes** **No** ☐		☐ **Yes** **No** ☐		☐ **Yes** **No** ☐	

GOALS: specific projects	Deadline Date	Days left?	Yes/No?
GOAL 1:			
GOAL 2:			

3 Wins of the Day

Daily Self Improvement (what did I learn today?)

Do I count today as a successful day? ☐ **Yes**   ☐ **No**

By the end of the day I want to be **a tiny bit better** than I was this morning || What have I <u>LEARNED</u> today || Don't Waste Time ||
<u>Make Yourself Into Something</u> || You're not everything you could be and you KNOW it || The #1 skill to develop is **COURAGE**

Date:	What Is My WHY?
Quote:	

Top Priority for Today		Top Priority for Tomorrow
	Achieved? ☐ Yes ☐ No If no – why?	

3 Daily Habits

Stretch		Gratitude		Hydrate	
Achieved?	Day nos:	Achieved?	Day nos:	Achieved?	Day nos:
☐ Yes No ☐		☐ Yes No ☐		☐ Yes No ☐	

GOALS: specific projects	Deadline Date	Days left?	Yes/No?
GOAL 1:			
GOAL 2:			

3 Wins of the Day

Daily Self Improvement (what did I learn today?)

Do I count today as a successful day? ☐ Yes ☐ No

By the end of the day I want to be **a tiny bit better** than I was this morning || What have I **LEARNED** today || Don't Waste Time ||
Make Yourself Into Something || You're not everything you could be and you KNOW it || The #1 skill to develop is **COURAGE**

Date:	What Is My WHY?
Quote:	

Top Priority for Today

	Achieved? ☐ Yes ☐ No If no – why?

Top Priority for Tomorrow

3 Daily Habits

Stretch		Gratitude		Hydrate	
Achieved?	Day nos:	Achieved?	Day nos:	Achieved?	Day nos:
☐ Yes No ☐		☐ Yes No ☐		☐ Yes No ☐	

GOALS: specific projects	Deadline Date	Days left?	Yes/No?
GOAL 1:			
GOAL 2:			

3 Wins of the Day

Daily Self Improvement (what did I learn today?)

Do I count today as a successful day? ☐ Yes ☐ No

By the end of the day I want to be **a tiny bit better** than I was this morning || What have I **LEARNED** today || Don't Waste Time ||

Make Yourself Into Something || You're not everything you could be and you KNOW it || The #1 skill to develop is **COURAGE**

Date:	What Is My WHY?
Quote:	

Top Priority for Today		Top Priority for Tomorrow
	Achieved? ☐ Yes ☐ No If no – why?	

3 Daily Habits

Stretch		Gratitude		Hydrate	
Achieved?	Day nos:	Achieved?	Day nos:	Achieved?	Day nos:
☐ Yes No ☐		☐ Yes No ☐		☐ Yes No ☐	

GOALS: specific projects	Deadline Date	Days left?	Yes/No?
GOAL 1:			
GOAL 2:			

3 Wins of the Day

Daily Self Improvement (what did I learn today?)

Do I count today as a successful day? ☐ Yes   ☐ No

By the end of the day I want to be **a tiny bit better** than I was this morning || What have I **LEARNED** today || Don't Waste Time ||
Make Yourself Into Something || You're not everything you could be and you KNOW it || The #1 skill to develop is **COURAGE**

Date:	What Is My WHY?
Quote:	

Top Priority for Today		Top Priority for Tomorrow
	Achieved? ☐ Yes ☐ No If no – why?	

3 Daily Habits

Stretch		Gratitude		Hydrate	
Achieved?	Day nos:	Achieved?	Day nos:	Achieved?	Day nos:
☐ Yes No ☐		☐ Yes No ☐		☐ Yes No ☐	

GOALS: specific projects	Deadline Date	Days left?	Yes/No?
GOAL 1:			
GOAL 2:			

3 Wins of the Day

Daily Self Improvement (what did I learn today?)

Do I count today as a successful day? ☐ Yes   ☐ No

By the end of the day I want to be **a tiny bit better** than I was this morning || What have I LEARNED today || Don't Waste Time || **Make Yourself Into Something** || You're not everything you could be and you KNOW it || The #1 skill to develop is **COURAGE**

Date:	What Is My WHY?
Quote:	

Top Priority for Today		Top Priority for Tomorrow
	Achieved? ☐ Yes ☐ No If no – why?	

3 Daily Habits

Stretch		Gratitude		Hydrate	
Achieved?	Day nos:	Achieved?	Day nos:	Achieved?	Day nos:
☐ Yes No ☐		☐ Yes No ☐		☐ Yes No ☐	

GOALS: specific projects	Deadline Date	Days left?	Yes/No?
GOAL 1:			
GOAL 2:			

3 Wins of the Day

Daily Self Improvement (what did I learn today?)

Do I count today as a successful day? ☐ Yes   ☐ No

By the end of the day I want to be **a tiny bit better** than I was this morning || What have I <u>LEARNED</u> today || Don't Waste Time ||
<u>Make Yourself Into Something</u> || You're not everything you could be and you KNOW it || The #1 skill to develop is **COURAGE**

Date:	What Is My WHY?
Quote:	

Top Priority for Today		Top Priority for Tomorrow
	Achieved? ☐ Yes ☐ No If no – why?	

3 Daily Habits

Stretch		Gratitude		Hydrate	
Achieved?	Day nos:	Achieved?	Day nos:	Achieved?	Day nos:
☐ Yes No ☐		☐ Yes No ☐		☐ Yes No ☐	

GOALS: specific projects	Deadline Date	Days left?	Yes/No?
GOAL 1:			
GOAL 2:			

3 Wins of the Day

Daily Self Improvement (what did I learn today?)

Do I count today as a successful day? ☐ Yes   ☐ No

By the end of the day I want to be **a tiny bit better** than I was this morning || What have I <u>LEARNED</u> today || Don't Waste Time || **Make Yourself Into Something** || You're not everything you could be and you KNOW it || The #1 skill to develop is **COURAGE**

Date:	What Is My WHY?
Quote:	

Top Priority for Today		Top Priority for Tomorrow
	Achieved? ☐ Yes ☐ No If no – why?	

3 Daily Habits

Stretch		Gratitude		Hydrate	
Achieved?	Day nos:	Achieved?	Day nos:	Achieved?	Day nos:
☐ Yes No ☐		☐ Yes No ☐		☐ Yes No ☐	

GOALS: specific projects	Deadline Date	Days left?	Yes/No?
GOAL 1:			
GOAL 2:			

3 Wins of the Day

Daily Self Improvement (what did I learn today?)

Do I count today as a successful day? ☐ Yes   ☐ No

By the end of the day I want to be **<u>a tiny bit better</u>** than I was this morning || What have I <u>**LEARNED**</u> today || Don't Waste Time || **<u>Make Yourself Into Something</u>** || You're not everything you could be and you KNOW it || The #1 skill to develop is **COURAGE**

Date:	What Is My WHY?
Quote:	

Top Priority for Today		Top Priority for Tomorrow
	Achieved? ☐ Yes ☐ No If no – why?	

3 Daily Habits

Stretch		Gratitude		Hydrate	
Achieved?	Day nos:	Achieved?	Day nos:	Achieved?	Day nos:
☐ Yes No ☐		☐ Yes No ☐		☐ Yes No ☐	

GOALS: specific projects	Deadline Date	Days left?	Yes/No?
GOAL 1:			
GOAL 2:			

3 Wins of the Day

Daily Self Improvement (what did I learn today?)

Do I count today as a successful day? ☐ Yes ☐ No

By the end of the day I want to be **a tiny bit better** than I was this morning || What have I <u>LEARNED</u> today || Don't Waste Time ||
Make Yourself Into Something || You're not everything you could be and you KNOW it || The #1 skill to develop is **COURAGE**

Date:		What Is My WHY?
Quote:		

Top Priority for Today | Top Priority for Tomorrow

Top Priority for Today	Achieved? ☐ Yes ☐ No If no – why?	

3 Daily Habits

Stretch		Gratitude		Hydrate	
Achieved?	Day nos:	Achieved?	Day nos:	Achieved?	Day nos:
☐ Yes No ☐		☐ Yes No ☐		☐ Yes No ☐	

GOALS: specific projects	Deadline Date	Days left?	Yes/No?
GOAL 1:			
GOAL 2:			

3 Wins of the Day

Daily Self Improvement (what did I learn today?)

Do I count today as a successful day? ☐ Yes ☐ No

By the end of the day I want to be **a tiny bit better** than I was this morning || What have I **LEARNED** today || Don't Waste Time ||
Make Yourself Into Something || You're not everything you could be and you KNOW it || The #1 skill to develop is **COURAGE**

Date:	What Is My WHY?
Quote:	

Top Priority for Today		Top Priority for Tomorrow
	Achieved? ☐ **Yes** ☐ **No** If no – why?	

3 Daily Habits

Stretch		Gratitude		Hydrate	
Achieved?	Day nos:	Achieved?	Day nos:	Achieved?	Day nos:
☐ **Yes** No ☐		☐ **Yes** No ☐		☐ **Yes** No ☐	

GOALS: specific projects	Deadline Date	Days left?	Yes/No?
GOAL 1:			
GOAL 2:			

3 Wins of the Day

Daily Self Improvement (what did I learn today?)

Do I count today as a successful day? ☐ Yes ☐ No

By the end of the day I want to be **a tiny bit better** than I was this morning || What have I <u>LEARNED</u> today || Don't Waste Time ||
Make Yourself Into Something || You're not everything you could be and you KNOW it || The #1 skill to develop is **COURAGE**

Date:		What Is My WHY?
Quote:		

Top Priority for Today		Top Priority for Tomorrow
	Achieved? ☐ Yes ☐ No If no – why?	

3 Daily Habits

Stretch		Gratitude		Hydrate	
Achieved?	Day nos:	Achieved?	Day nos:	Achieved?	Day nos:
☐ Yes No ☐		☐ Yes No ☐		☐ Yes No ☐	

GOALS: specific projects	Deadline Date	Days left?	Yes/No?
GOAL 1:			
GOAL 2:			

3 Wins of the Day

Daily Self Improvement (what did I learn today?)

Do I count today as a successful day? ☐ Yes ☐ No

By the end of the day I want to be **a tiny bit better** than I was this morning || What have I **LEARNED** today || Don't Waste Time ||
Make Yourself Into Something || You're not everything you could be and you KNOW it || The #1 skill to develop is **COURAGE**

Date:	What Is My WHY?
Quote:	

Top Priority for Today		Top Priority for Tomorrow
	Achieved? ☐ **Yes** ☐ **No** If no – why?	

3 Daily Habits

Stretch		Gratitude		Hydrate	
Achieved?	**Day nos:**	**Achieved?**	**Day nos:**	**Achieved?**	**Day nos:**
☐ **Yes** No ☐		☐ **Yes** No ☐		☐ **Yes** No ☐	

GOALS: specific projects	Deadline Date	Days left?	Yes/No?
GOAL 1:			
GOAL 2:			

3 Wins of the Day

Daily Self Improvement (what did I learn today?)

	Do I count today as a successful day? ☐ Yes ☐ No

By the end of the day I want to be **a tiny bit better** than I was this morning || What have I <u>LEARNED</u> today || Don't Waste Time ||
<u>Make Yourself Into Something</u> || You're not everything you could be and you KNOW it || The #1 skill to develop is **COURAGE**

Date:	What Is My WHY?
Quote:	

Top Priority for Today		Top Priority for Tomorrow
	Achieved? ☐ **Yes** ☐ **No** If no – why?	

3 Daily Habits

Stretch		Gratitude		Hydrate	
Achieved?	Day nos:	Achieved?	Day nos:	Achieved?	Day nos:
☐ **Yes** No ☐		☐ **Yes** No ☐		☐ **Yes** No ☐	

GOALS: specific projects	Deadline Date	Days left?	Yes/No?
GOAL 1:			
GOAL 2:			

3 Wins of the Day

Daily Self Improvement (what did I learn today?)

Do I count today as a successful day? ☐ Yes   ☐ No

By the end of the day I want to be **a tiny bit better** than I was this morning || What have I **LEARNED** today || Don't Waste Time ||
Make Yourself Into Something || You're not everything you could be and you KNOW it || The #1 skill to develop is **COURAGE**

Date:	What Is My WHY?
Quote:	

Top Priority for Today		Top Priority for Tomorrow
	Achieved? ☐ **Yes** ☐ No If no – why?	

3 Daily Habits

Stretch		Gratitude		Hydrate	
Achieved?	Day nos:	Achieved?	Day nos:	Achieved?	Day nos:
☐ **Yes** No ☐		☐ **Yes** No ☐		☐ **Yes** No ☐	

GOALS: specific projects	Deadline Date	Days left?	Yes/No?
GOAL 1:			
GOAL 2:			

3 Wins of the Day

Daily Self Improvement (what did I learn today?)

Do I count today as a successful day? ☐ Yes ☐ No

By the end of the day I want to be **a tiny bit better** than I was this morning || What have I <u>LEARNED</u> today || Don't Waste Time || **Make Yourself Into Something** || You're not everything you could be and you KNOW it || The #1 skill to develop is **COURAGE**

Date:	What Is My WHY?
Quote:	

Top Priority for Today		Top Priority for Tomorrow
	Achieved? ☐ **Yes** ☐ **No** If no – why?	

3 Daily Habits

Stretch		Gratitude		Hydrate	
Achieved?	Day nos:	Achieved?	Day nos:	Achieved?	Day nos:
☐ **Yes** No ☐		☐ **Yes** No ☐		☐ **Yes** No ☐	

GOALS: specific projects	Deadline Date	Days left?	Yes/No?
GOAL 1:			
GOAL 2:			

3 Wins of the Day

Daily Self Improvement (what did I learn today?)

Do I count today as a successful day? ☐ Yes ☐ No

By the end of the day I want to be **a tiny bit better** than I was this morning || What have I **LEARNED** today || Don't Waste Time ||
Make Yourself Into Something || You're not everything you could be and you KNOW it || The #1 skill to develop is **COURAGE**

Date:	What Is My WHY?
Quote:	

Top Priority for Today | Top Priority for Tomorrow

	Achieved? ☐ **Yes** ☐ **No** If no – why?	

3 Daily Habits

Stretch		Gratitude		Hydrate	
Achieved?	Day nos:	Achieved?	Day nos:	Achieved?	Day nos:
☐ **Yes** No ☐		☐ **Yes** No ☐		☐ **Yes** No ☐	

GOALS: specific projects	Deadline Date	Days left?	Yes/No?
GOAL 1:			
GOAL 2:			

3 Wins of the Day

Daily Self Improvement (what did I learn today?)

Do I count today as a successful day? ☐ Yes   ☐ No

By the end of the day I want to be **a tiny bit better** than I was this morning || What have I <u>LEARNED</u> today || Don't Waste Time ||

Make Yourself Into Something || You're not everything you could be and you KNOW it || The #1 skill to develop is **COURAGE**

Date:		What Is My WHY?
Quote:		

Top Priority for Today		Top Priority for Tomorrow
	Achieved? ☐ **Yes** ☐ **No** If no – why?	

3 Daily Habits

Stretch		Gratitude		Hydrate	
Achieved?	**Day nos:**	**Achieved?**	**Day nos:**	**Achieved?**	**Day nos:**
☐ **Yes** No ☐		☐ **Yes** No ☐		☐ **Yes** No ☐	

GOALS: specific projects	Deadline Date	Days left?	Yes/No?
GOAL 1:			
GOAL 2:			

3 Wins of the Day

Daily Self Improvement (what did I learn today?)

Do I count today as a successful day? ☐ Yes   ☐ No

By the end of the day I want to be **a tiny bit better** than I was this morning || What have I **LEARNED** today || Don't Waste Time ||

Make Yourself Into Something || You're not everything you could be and you KNOW it || The #1 skill to develop is **COURAGE**

Date:	What Is My WHY?
Quote:	

Top Priority for Today		Top Priority for Tomorrow
	Achieved? ☐ Yes ☐ No If no – why?	

3 Daily Habits

Stretch		Gratitude		Hydrate	
Achieved?	Day nos:	Achieved?	Day nos:	Achieved?	Day nos:
☐ Yes No ☐		☐ Yes No ☐		☐ Yes No ☐	

GOALS: specific projects	Deadline Date	Days left?	Yes/No?
GOAL 1:			
GOAL 2:			

3 Wins of the Day

Daily Self Improvement (what did I learn today?)

Do I count today as a successful day? ☐ Yes ☐ No

By the end of the day I want to be **a tiny bit better** than I was this morning || What have I <u>LEARNED</u> today || Don't Waste Time ||
Make Yourself Into Something || You're not everything you could be and you KNOW it || The #1 skill to develop is **COURAGE**

Date:	What Is My WHY?
Quote:	

Top Priority for Today		Top Priority for Tomorrow
	Achieved? ☐ **Yes** ☐ **No** If no – why?	

3 Daily Habits

Stretch		Gratitude		Hydrate	
Achieved?	Day nos:	Achieved?	Day nos:	Achieved?	Day nos:
☐ **Yes** No ☐		☐ **Yes** No ☐		☐ **Yes** No ☐	

GOALS: specific projects	Deadline Date	Days left?	Yes/No?
GOAL 1:			
GOAL 2:			

3 Wins of the Day

Daily Self Improvement (what did I learn today?)

Do I count today as a successful day? ☐ Yes ☐ No

By the end of the day I want to be **a tiny bit better** than I was this morning || What have I **LEARNED** today || Don't Waste Time ||
Make Yourself Into Something || You're not everything you could be and you KNOW it || The #1 skill to develop is **COURAGE**

Date:	What Is My WHY?
Quote:	

Top Priority for Today		Top Priority for Tomorrow
	Achieved? ☐ Yes ☐ No If no – why?	

3 Daily Habits

Stretch		Gratitude		Hydrate	
Achieved?	Day nos:	Achieved?	Day nos:	Achieved?	Day nos:
☐ Yes No ☐		☐ Yes No ☐		☐ Yes No ☐	

GOALS: specific projects	Deadline Date	Days left?	Yes/No?
GOAL 1:			
GOAL 2:			

3 Wins of the Day

Daily Self Improvement (what did I learn today?)

Do I count today as a successful day? ☐ Yes   ☐ No

By the end of the day I want to be **a tiny bit better** than I was this morning || What have I LEARNED today || Don't Waste Time ||
Make Yourself Into Something || You're not everything you could be and you KNOW it || The #1 skill to develop is **COURAGE**

Date:	What Is My WHY?
Quote:	

Top Priority for Today | Top Priority for Tomorrow

	Achieved? ☐ Yes ☐ No If no – why?	

3 Daily Habits

Stretch		Gratitude		Hydrate	
Achieved?	Day nos:	Achieved?	Day nos:	Achieved?	Day nos
☐ Yes No ☐		☐ Yes No ☐		☐ Yes No ☐	

GOALS: specific projects	Deadline Date	Days left?	Yes/No?
GOAL 1:			
GOAL 2:			

3 Wins of the Day

Daily Self Improvement (what did I learn today?)

Do I count today as a successful day? ☐ Yes ☐ No

By the end of the day I want to be **a tiny bit better** than I was this morning || What have I <u>LEARNED</u> today || Don't Waste Time ||
<u>Make Yourself Into Something</u> || You're not everything you could be and you KNOW it || The #1 skill to develop is **COURAGE**

Date:	What Is My WHY?
Quote:	

Top Priority for Today

	Achieved? ☐ Yes ☐ No If no – why?

Top Priority for Tomorrow

3 Daily Habits

Stretch		Gratitude		Hydrate	
Achieved?	Day nos:	Achieved?	Day nos:	Achieved?	Day nos:
☐ Yes No ☐		☐ Yes No ☐		☐ Yes No ☐	

GOALS: specific projects

	Deadline Date	Days left?	Yes/No?
GOAL 1:			
GOAL 2:			

3 Wins of the Day

Daily Self Improvement (what did I learn today?)

Do I count today as a successful day? ☐ Yes ☐ No

By the end of the day I want to be **a tiny bit better** than I was this morning || What have I LEARNED today || Don't Waste Time ||
Make Yourself Into Something || You're not everything you could be and you KNOW it || The #1 skill to develop is COURAGE

Date:	What Is My WHY?
Quote:	

Top Priority for Today		Top Priority for Tomorrow
	Achieved? ☐ Yes ☐ No If no – why?	

3 Daily Habits

Stretch		Gratitude		Hydrate	
Achieved?	Day nos:	Achieved?	Day nos:	Achieved?	Day nos:
☐ Yes No ☐		☐ Yes No ☐		☐ Yes No ☐	

GOALS: specific projects	Deadline Date	Days left?	Yes/No?
GOAL 1:			
GOAL 2:			

3 Wins of the Day

Daily Self Improvement (what did I learn today?)

Do I count today as a successful day? ☐ Yes ☐ No

By the end of the day I want to be **a tiny bit better** than I was this morning || What have I **LEARNED** today || Don't Waste Time || **Make Yourself Into Something** || You're not everything you could be and you KNOW it || The #1 skill to develop is **COURAGE**

Date:	What Is My WHY?
Quote:	

Top Priority for Today		Top Priority for Tomorrow
	Achieved? ☐ Yes ☐ No If no – why?	

3 Daily Habits

Stretch		Gratitude		Hydrate	
Achieved?	Day nos:	Achieved?	Day nos:	Achieved?	Day nos:
☐ Yes No ☐		☐ Yes No ☐		☐ Yes No ☐	

GOALS: specific projects	Deadline Date	Days left?	Yes/No?
GOAL 1:			
GOAL 2:			

3 Wins of the Day

Daily Self Improvement (what did I learn today?)

Do I count today as a successful day? ☐ Yes   ☐ No

By the end of the day I want to be **a tiny bit better** than I was this morning || What have I <u>LEARNED</u> today || Don't Waste Time ||
<u>Make Yourself Into Something</u> || You're not everything you could be and you KNOW it || The #1 skill to develop is **COURAGE**

Date:	What Is My WHY?
Quote:	

Top Priority for Today		Top Priority for Tomorrow
	Achieved? ☐ Yes ☐ No If no – why?	

3 Daily Habits

Stretch		Gratitude		Hydrate	
Achieved?	Day nos:	Achieved?	Day nos:	Achieved?	Day nos:
☐ Yes No ☐		☐ Yes No ☐		☐ Yes No ☐	

GOALS: specific projects	Deadline Date	Days left?	Yes/No?
GOAL 1:			
GOAL 2:			

3 Wins of the Day

Daily Self Improvement (what did I learn today?)

Do I count today as a successful day? ☐ Yes ☐ No

By the end of the day I want to be **a tiny bit better** than I was this morning || What have I **LEARNED** today || Don't Waste Time ||
Make Yourself Into Something || You're not everything you could be and you KNOW it || The #1 skill to develop is **COURAGE**

Date:	What Is My WHY?
Quote:	

Top Priority for Today | Top Priority for Tomorrow

	Achieved? ☐ **Yes** ☐ **No** If no – why?	

3 Daily Habits

Stretch		Gratitude		Hydrate	
Achieved?	Day nos:	Achieved?	Day nos:	Achieved?	Day nos:
☐ Yes No ☐		☐ Yes No ☐		☐ Yes No ☐	

GOALS: specific projects | Deadline Date | Days left? | Yes/No?

	Deadline Date	Days left?	Yes/No?
GOAL 1:			
GOAL 2:			

3 Wins of the Day

Daily Self Improvement (what did I learn today?)

Do I count today as a successful day? ☐ Yes ☐ No

By the end of the day I want to be **a tiny bit better** than I was this morning || What have I <u>LEARNED</u> today || Don't Waste Time || **Make Yourself Into Something** || You're not everything you could be and you KNOW it || The #1 skill to develop is **COURAGE**

Date:	What Is My WHY?
Quote:	

Top Priority for Today		Top Priority for Tomorrow
	Achieved? ☐ **Yes** ☐ **No** If no – why?	

3 Daily Habits					
Stretch		**Gratitude**		**Hydrate**	
Achieved?	Day nos:	Achieved?	Day nos:	Achieved?	Day nos:
☐ **Yes** No ☐		☐ **Yes** No ☐		☐ **Yes** No ☐	

GOALS: specific projects	Deadline Date	Days left?	Yes/No?
GOAL 1:			
GOAL 2:			

3 Wins of the Day		

Daily Self Improvement (what did I learn today?)

Do I count today as a successful day? ☐ Yes ☐ No

By the end of the day I want to be **a tiny bit better** than I was this morning || What have I **LEARNED** today || Don't Waste Time ||
Make Yourself Into Something || You're not everything you could be and you KNOW it || The #1 skill to develop is **COURAGE**

Date:	What Is My WHY?
Quote:	

Top Priority for Today		Top Priority for Tomorrow
	Achieved? ☐ **Yes** ☐ **No** If no – why?	

3 Daily Habits

Stretch		Gratitude		Hydrate	
Achieved?	**Day nos:**	**Achieved?**	**Day nos:**	**Achieved?**	**Day nos:**
☐ **Yes** No ☐		☐ **Yes** No ☐		☐ **Yes** No ☐	

GOALS: specific projects	Deadline Date	Days left?	Yes/No?
GOAL 1:			
GOAL 2:			

3 Wins of the Day

Daily Self Improvement (what did I learn today?)

Do I count today as a successful day? ☐ Yes ☐ No

By the end of the day I want to be **a tiny bit better** than I was this morning || What have I LEARNED today || Don't Waste Time ||
Make Yourself Into Something || You're not everything you could be and you KNOW it || The #1 skill to develop is **COURAGE**

Date:	What Is My WHY?
Quote:	

Top Priority for Today		Top Priority for Tomorrow
	Achieved? ☐ **Yes** ☐ **No** If no – why?	

3 Daily Habits

Stretch		Gratitude		Hydrate	
Achieved?	Day nos:	Achieved?	Day nos:	Achieved?	Day nos:
☐ **Yes** No ☐		☐ **Yes** No ☐		☐ **Yes** No ☐	

GOALS: specific projects	Deadline Date	Days left?	Yes/No?
GOAL 1:			
GOAL 2:			

3 Wins of the Day

Daily Self Improvement (what did I learn today?)

Do I count today as a successful day? ☐ Yes ☐ No

By the end of the day I want to be **a tiny bit better** than I was this morning || What have I **LEARNED** today || Don't Waste Time ||
Make Yourself Into Something || You're not everything you could be and you KNOW it || The #1 skill to develop is **COURAGE**

Date:	What Is My WHY?
Quote:	

Top Priority for Today		Top Priority for Tomorrow
	Achieved? ☐ Yes ☐ No If no – why?	

3 Daily Habits

Stretch		Gratitude		Hydrate	
Achieved?	Day nos:	Achieved?	Day nos:	Achieved?	Day nos:
☐ Yes No ☐		☐ Yes No ☐		☐ Yes No ☐	

GOALS: specific projects	Deadline Date	Days left?	Yes/No?
GOAL 1:			
GOAL 2:			

3 Wins of the Day

Daily Self Improvement (what did I learn today?)

Do I count today as a successful day? ☐ Yes ☐ No

By the end of the day I want to be **a tiny bit better** than I was this morning || What have I <u>LEARNED</u> today || Don't Waste Time ||
<u>Make Yourself Into Something</u> || You're not everything you could be and you KNOW it || The #1 skill to develop is **COURAGE**

Date:		What Is My WHY?
Quote:		

Top Priority for Today | | ## Top Priority for Tomorrow

Top Priority for Today	Achieved? ☐ **Yes** ☐ **No** If no – why?	Top Priority for Tomorrow

3 Daily Habits

Stretch		Gratitude		Hydrate	
Achieved?	Day nos:	Achieved?	Day nos:	Achieved?	Day nos:
☐ **Yes** No ☐		☐ **Yes** No ☐		☐ **Yes** No ☐	

GOALS: specific projects	Deadline Date	Days left?	Yes/No?
GOAL 1:			
GOAL 2:			

3 Wins of the Day

Daily Self Improvement (what did I learn today?)

Do I count today as a successful day? ☐ Yes   ☐ No

By the end of the day I want to be **a tiny bit better** than I was this morning || What have I **LEARNED** today || Don't Waste Time ||
Make Yourself Into Something || You're not everything you could be and you KNOW it || The #1 skill to develop is **COURAGE**

Date:	What Is My WHY?
Quote:	

Top Priority for Today		Top Priority for Tomorrow
	Achieved? ☐ **Yes** ☐ **No** If no – why?	

3 Daily Habits

Stretch		Gratitude		Hydrate	
Achieved?	Day nos:	Achieved?	Day nos:	Achieved?	Day nos:
☐ **Yes** No ☐		☐ **Yes** No ☐		☐ **Yes** No ☐	

GOALS: specific projects	Deadline Date	Days left?	Yes/No?
GOAL 1:			
GOAL 2:			

3 Wins of the Day

Daily Self Improvement (what did I learn today?)

Do I count today as a successful day? ☐ Yes ☐ No

By the end of the day I want to be **a tiny bit better** than I was this morning || What have I <u>LEARNED</u> today || Don't Waste Time ||
Make Yourself Into Something || You're not everything you could be and you KNOW it || The #1 skill to develop is **COURAGE**

Date:	What Is My WHY?
Quote:	

Top Priority for Today		Top Priority for Tomorrow
	Achieved? ☐ **Yes** ☐ **No** If no – why?	

3 Daily Habits

Stretch		Gratitude		Hydrate	
Achieved?	Day nos:	Achieved?	Day nos:	Achieved?	Day nos:
☐ **Yes** No ☐		☐ **Yes** No ☐		☐ **Yes** No ☐	

GOALS: specific projects	Deadline Date	Days left?	Yes/No?
GOAL 1:			
GOAL 2:			

3 Wins of the Day

Daily Self Improvement (what did I learn today?)

Do I count today as a successful day? ☐ Yes ☐ No

By the end of the day I want to be **a tiny bit better** than I was this morning || What have I **LEARNED** today || Don't Waste Time ||
Make Yourself Into Something || You're not everything you could be and you KNOW it || The #1 skill to develop is **COURAGE**

Date:	What Is My WHY?
Quote:	

Top Priority for Today		Top Priority for Tomorrow
	Achieved? ☐ **Yes** ☐ No If no – why?	

3 Daily Habits

Stretch		Gratitude		Hydrate	
Achieved?	Day nos:	Achieved?	Day nos:	Achieved?	Day nos:
☐ **Yes** No ☐		☐ **Yes** No ☐		☐ **Yes** No ☐	

GOALS: specific projects	Deadline Date	Days left?	Yes/No?
GOAL 1:			
GOAL 2:			

3 Wins of the Day

Daily Self Improvement (what did I learn today?)

	Do I count today as a successful day? ☐ Yes ☐ No

By the end of the day I want to be **a tiny bit better** than I was this morning || What have I <u>LEARNED</u> today || Don't Waste Time ||
<u>Make Yourself Into Something</u> || You're not everything you could be and you KNOW it || The #1 skill to develop is **COURAGE**

Date:	What Is My WHY?
Quote:	

Top Priority for Today		Top Priority for Tomorrow
	Achieved? ☐ Yes ☐ No If no – why?	

3 Daily Habits

Stretch		Gratitude		Hydrate	
Achieved?	Day nos:	Achieved?	Day nos:	Achieved?	Day nos:
☐ Yes No ☐		☐ Yes No ☐		☐ Yes No ☐	

GOALS: specific projects	Deadline Date	Days left?	Yes/No?
GOAL 1:			
GOAL 2:			

3 Wins of the Day

Daily Self Improvement (what did I learn today?)

Do I count today as a successful day? ☐ Yes ☐ No

By the end of the day I want to be **a tiny bit better** than I was this morning || What have I **LEARNED** today || Don't Waste Time ||

Make Yourself Into Something || You're not everything you could be and you KNOW it || The #1 skill to develop is **COURAGE**

Date:	What Is My WHY?
Quote:	

Top Priority for Today		Top Priority for Tomorrow
	Achieved? ☐ Yes ☐ No If no – why?	

3 Daily Habits

Stretch		Gratitude		Hydrate	
Achieved?	Day nos:	Achieved?	Day nos:	Achieved?	Day nos:
☐ Yes No ☐		☐ Yes No ☐		☐ Yes No ☐	

GOALS: specific projects	Deadline Date	Days left?	Yes/No?
GOAL 1:			
GOAL 2:			

3 Wins of the Day

Daily Self Improvement (what did I learn today?)

Do I count today as a successful day? ☐ Yes ☐ No

By the end of the day I want to be **a tiny bit better** than I was this morning || What have I LEARNED today || Don't Waste Time ||
Make Yourself Into Something || You're not everything you could be and you KNOW it || The #1 skill to develop is **COURAGE**

Date:	What Is My WHY?
Quote:	

Top Priority for Today		Top Priority for Tomorrow
	Achieved? ☐ Yes ☐ No If no – why?	

3 Daily Habits

Stretch		Gratitude		Hydrate	
Achieved?	Day nos:	Achieved?	Day nos:	Achieved?	Day nos:
☐ Yes No ☐		☐ Yes No ☐		☐ Yes No ☐	

GOALS: specific projects	Deadline Date	Days left?	Yes/No?
GOAL 1:			
GOAL 2:			

3 Wins of the Day

Daily Self Improvement (what did I learn today?)

Do I count today as a successful day? ☐ Yes   ☐ No

By the end of the day I want to be **a tiny bit better** than I was this morning || What have I **LEARNED** today || Don't Waste Time ||
Make Yourself Into Something || You're not everything you could be and you KNOW it || The #1 skill to develop is **COURAGE**

Date:	What Is My WHY?
Quote:	

Top Priority for Today		Top Priority for Tomorrow
	Achieved? ☐ **Yes** ☐ **No** If no – why?	

3 Daily Habits

Stretch		Gratitude		Hydrate	
Achieved?	Day nos:	Achieved?	Day nos:	Achieved?	Day nos:
☐ **Yes** No ☐		☐ **Yes** No ☐		☐ **Yes** No ☐	

GOALS: specific projects	Deadline Date	Days left?	Yes/No?
GOAL 1:			
GOAL 2:			

3 Wins of the Day

Daily Self Improvement (what did I learn today?)

Do I count today as a successful day? ☐ Yes ☐ No

By the end of the day I want to be **a tiny bit better** than I was this morning || What have I <u>LEARNED</u> today || Don't Waste Time ||
Make Yourself Into Something || You're not everything you could be and you KNOW it || The #1 skill to develop is **COURAGE**

Printed in Great Britain
by Amazon

80057238R00038